Lessons I've Learned

From

A Flower

Lessons I've Learned From A Flower

Joan M. Scharff

For information, address Running Quail Press, Inc., PO Box 5274, Peoria, AZ 85385-5274.

ISBN: 978-0-9840331-7-1

Printed in the United States of America
First Edition

Cover Design by Joan M. Scharff
Photographs by Joan M. Scharff

Back Cover Photo of Author by Jacqueline Karl Ferrell

Additional photographs used with permission by:

Jacqueline Karl Ferrell
Michelle Parsons
Catherine Scharff
and Jerri Weigand

"The earth laughs in flowers."
- Ralph Waldo Emerson

"Yet to pursue a purpose in life so
strenuously
that you will not linger
among its flowers,
is to miss the best of all."
- Donald Culross Peattie

This book is lovingly dedicated to my family; and to the people and the presence that shaped it. I give special thanks to God, the Master Gardener.

Written also with special honor to Shaun, for her loving and inspiring spirit; and to each of the people she loved and connected with her presence. As Shaun bravely shared her personal journey of adversity and experience of breast cancer; she found each moment's blessing —reminding us we can too. Thanks to Shaun, and her brave and unending pursuit of dreams and infinite possibilities, and for all the beautiful flowers and inspirations in my life. You are unforgettable and loved.

Photograph by Cathy Scharff

Introduction

Life is about the connections we make, share and develop. My life is blessed because of my connection to Joan Scharff. I met Joan a few years ago at a networking event. I remember her as quiet, perhaps even a bit timid, though with the creative glow of a flame ready to light up the world for others. When I saw her breathtaking photos and inspirational thoughts, I realized the flame was more like a budding flower, peeking out through its petals, waiting for the right moment to dazzle everyone with its empowering bloom. Joan, you are in full bloom! It gives me great pleasure to endorse this delightful book which is truly a glorious work of art inspired by a connection to nature, and nurtured along by our dear friend, the late Shaun Stephenson.

Marilyn Kleinberg

Founder, eWomenNetwork Southern New Jersey

President, Empowering Connections

Honor
the teachers in your life.
Be grateful for their
generosity and mastery.

Cactus Flower, *Echinopsis Ferox*
Lobivia longispina

Photograph by Cathy Scharff

We each have
something to contribute.
Be the best you can be
and serve others.

Blanket Flower
Gaillardia aristata

Diversity makes us
interesting. Often our
differences compliment
each other.

Lily, *Lilium*
Montbretia, *Masoniorium crocosmia*
Feathered Amaranth, *Celosia argenta*

Look Up.
Expand your perspective.

Flowering Dogwood Tree
Cornus florida

It's okay to be a little different.
Sometimes it's the very thing
that makes you unforgettable.

Forget-Me-Not
Myosotis sylvatica

Reach for the Sun.
With all of your energy, seek the
Power that opens and fulfills you.

Zucchini, Summer Squash
Cucubuta pepo

A flower is evidence
that something
extraordinary and beautiful
can emerge from a dark place.
Never give up.

Waterlilly
Nymphaea

Be as bright and beautiful
as you can be.

Sour Cherry Blossom
Prunus cerasus

Anything can happen.

Adria Bellflower
Campanula portenschlagiana

Sometimes we have to get through the muck and mire before we see the sunshine again.
Bask; don't miss the beautiful reflection of the angels around you.

Waterlilly
Nymphaea

A little fragrance
goes a long way.

Lilac
Syringa spp.

It's okay to be funky.

Passion Flower
Passiflora

Open and Attract.
Do your own work and
experience the magic.

Yellow Hibiscus
Hibiscus rosa-sinensis

Even a soft and beautiful
rose has thorns.
Be humble and grateful.

Rose
Rosa

The beauty of a flower
is like the
caring and kindness
of a friend.
Both have a long lasting effect
on the heart.

Lisianthus
Eustoma grandiflorum

Photograph by Michelle Parsons

Kind, gentle truth
and presence are
powerful.

Southern Magnolia
Magnolia grandiflora

We all need some rain.

Bearded Iris
Iris hybrida

Good things come in all
shapes and sizes.

Dwarf Crested Iris
Iris cristata

If life strips you of your petals,
stand tall anyway.

Sunflower
Helianthus annuus

Be Resilient.
Show up.
Even in the dark and rocky
places, seek to brighten
someone's day.

Nodding Beggarticks
Bidens cernua

It's fun to be part of a bunch.

English Daisy
Bellis perennis

We need each other.

Moon Flower
Datura stramonium

Sometimes the shadows
reveal
interesting surprises and
other dimensions.

Azalea
Rhododendron indicum

We all need
support and protection.

Sunflower
Helianthus annus

What a difference
a day can make.

Christmas Cactus
Schlumbergera bridesii

Pay attention.
There is always
another angle.

Christmas Cactus
Schlumbergera bridesii

You don't always have to be the center of attention.
Let others shine.

Variegated Vinca
Vinca major "variegata"

Set the stage.
First impressions are welcoming.

Primrose
Primula vulgaris

It's okay to be a little shy.

Pansy
Viola wittrockiana

Let the Light shine through
and remember the Source.

Chrysanthemum
Dendranthema grandiflora

Happiness rubs off.

Profusion Zinnia
Zinnia elegans

Take time to hang
out with others.

Bluebell
Hyacinthoides non-scripta

A little mist never hurt anyone.

Bachelor's Buttons /Japanese Rose
Kerria japonica

Breathe in the wonder and glory.

Crab Apple Tree
Malus X robusta 'Red Sentinel'

The wind on your face feels good.
Go with the flow.
Dance and wiggle
along with life.

Red Corn Poppy
Papaver rhoeas

Dancing with others
is a blast.

Shasta Daisy
Leucanthemum x superbum

Wild can be amazing.

Ground Ivy
Glechoma hederacea

Sometimes
you fall face down
in the dirt.

Columbine
Aquilegia caerulea krystal

Even with our differences,
there is much the
same about us.

Firecracker Sunflower
Helianthus annuus

Everyone has
star-like qualities.
Look for and nurture them.

Hollyhock
Alcea

Together we are
bigger and stronger.
We can accomplish more.
How blessed to have a
network and team to rely on.

Old Fashioned Snowball Bush
Viburnum, Opulus roseum

Despite differences,
love and appreciate
family and friends.
Accept people as they are
(we're all a little fruity).

Chrysanthemum
Chrysanthemum indicum
Pumpkin
Cucurbita maxima

Photograph by Jerri Weigand
Words Inspired by Eeelizabanana

Wait your turn.

Clematis Clair de Lune
Clematis evirin

Remember the view
from grass level.
Don't step on the little things.

Common Lawn Daisy
Bellis perennis

Care for and coexist with
all living things.

Dogwood Tree
Cornus florida
Robin
Turdus migratorius

There are various phases
of development.
It's okay to be where you are.

Flowering Dogwood Tree
Cornus florida

Don't be afraid
to stretch and stand out.

Flowering Dogwood Tree
Cornus florida

Zoom in to take a
closer look at the
heart of magnificence!

Flowering Dogwood Tree
Cornus florida

Wilting happens.
Rest and restoration
are necessary parts of the
cycle of life.

Flowering Dogwood Tree
Cornus florida

Joy is everywhere.

Chrysanthemum
Dendranthema grandiflora

You are never alone.

Chrysanthemum
Dendranthema grandiflora

Don't overlook the small things.
Seemingly small things
often have great significance.
Give them a chance.
Look twice.

Chrysanthemum
Dendranthema grandiflora

You are loved despite
your bumps and flaws.

Wild Cherry
Prunus avium

Be peaceful...
like a long deep breath,
a gentle mountain breeze,
and the joy and calm feeling
a flower brings.

Colorado Blue Columbine
Aquilegia caerulea

Photograph by Cathy Scharff

Risk it. Go first.
The world needs leaders.

Round-leaved Cranesbill
Geranium rotundisolium

A little dirt on the face
never hurt anyone.

Primrose
Primula vulgaris

There are no accidents.

Dandelion
Taraxacum

Today's seeds
are tomorrow's flowers.
Collect and plant them for
fate favors the prepared.

Purple Cone Flower
Echinacea angustifolia

Photograph by Jacqueline Karl Ferrell

Integrity
and
honor matter.

Peony
Paeonia

Don't let a blemish
hold you back.

Tulip
Tulipa

It's okay to
stand apart
from the crowd.

Obedient Plant
Physotegia virginiana

Be Inspired.
Look beyond the obvious.
Every moment has purpose,
and each experience has scope.

Hollyhock
Alcea

Look inside.

Camellia
Camellia sasanqua

Some things stay around

for generations.

Flowering Dogwood Tree
Cornus florida

Simply
love
more.

Black Eyed Susan
Rudbeckia hirta

Spring Rain

The morning after spring rain
Not a single rose bud; not yet.
Each leaf surrounded

Enveloped by tiny drops
Micro beads of rain caught in light
As if to say we are here

All around you
Just what you need now
Gift of spring rain

Dorothy of 17 Bluebell

Ninety one years young she is
Dorothy of 17 Bluebell
Out for her daily walk on a blustery winter's day
Body young wearing black sweatpants and a red hoodie
A vessel visibly cared for
Red hood over faux fur hat
Covers all but a wisp of grey and brittle hair
Brows wild, unnoticed now
A small sign of ninety one years
Red lipstick and dark glasses
Tells stories of life's twists and turns
Love found and love lost
Of beautiful endings and beginnings
Undying faith
Of spending days with God and her Rosary
In the divine company of Chloe the Cat

Petals

Scatter in the wind like possibilities
Pink flecks fly freely
Fall through the air and land like snow
On rooftops and ground below
Settle into garden beds
Cherry Blossom remnants
Depart from the place they began
Do they know?

So many petals, once together as one
Fly away too soon
Leave me wanting
To gather and keep them
As if I could
Until the time they come again

Perhaps I'll do the only thing I can
To say goodbye and thank them
For the beauty
For the pleasure
For the flowering moments
For their life as it touched mine

One Beating Heart

One need not look too far to remember
Look to the sky, the formation of clouds, the varying colors
Look to the landscapes and the seasons
Look to the many different winged ones who fly through
the clear open blue
No two created exactly the same
Each tree unique, standing in its own place.
Every flower with its individual beauty and fragrance
Opening in its perfect time
Yet all this life touched by one sun
Connected and rooted in this same round earth
One beating heart
What if there was only one dance, one song, one point of view?
Imagine this, if in a blink of an eye, you opened to see only
one color, one form.
Where would you be?
Would you even recognize yourself?
Would you be large or small?
Would the world be white or black, red or yellow?

Fallen Petals

When honor and integrity fall prey to fear
Hearts break and fall too
Like the petals of an aging flower
Once glorious, whole, alive
Once seeking the light of the sun
Truly beautiful with Godly fragrance
Petals fall and scatter
When mistakes and choices are made, guided by fear and shame
In split seconds, integrity is lost to false securities
Hearts scatter like the fallen petals on the wind
Drift and separate from leaf and stem
Only faint remembrance of the sweet aroma
When we turn passively from truth, afraid to see and acknowledge its discomfort
Hearts fall captive, shadows and clouds cover the sunlight
Yet, truth is meant to be followed
It takes courage and honor to speak and face it
To speak the unspeakable
To look squarely at it and cast a light upon it
Truth holds the power to stop harm; to open a door to justice, to have us face our mistakes
What is it that we are called to be in the moment of truth?
Who is our true Judge?

Can honest tears fall freely, cleansing the passion and
desire for vengeance?
Will our eyes be awakened to greater love and
acceptance?
Will our hearts, like the fallen petals in the wind take flight
again?

May the goodness and honor of one lost, transform the
heart of another's shame
May God's Grace and Mercy soften and set free our
dampened spirits
Dancing, once again like fallen petals in the wind, gently
spreading the fragrance of redemption

This Old Fence

This old fence
Illuminated by the sun
Shadow caught my eye and drew me in.
It has seen better days for sure
Stand a moment reminded of all the work to be done, and
wonder
How will I manage the larger tasks? Who might I call to
help me with this work?
This old fence, clinging to the vines that live upon it
They may be the only strength it knows now, seems they
hold it up
Notice the light and grasp life's green vibrancy even in the
dead of winter
This old fence, loyally it has served its purpose
Worn broken wood; bug eaten tracks, decayed and near
collapse in places, though still
I love it and what it offers
It stretches over the landscape of this old home
Providing a place for the Climbing Hydrangea to live and
bloom
A path for squirrel to travel atop, to pause and eat its nut
in safety
A resting perch for Cardinal, Wren and Dragonfly

It reminds me gratefully of the others who worked and walked along its boundary

Remember them as I gaze through a hole on a snowy day and watch in wonderment as a Junko finds food in the early light

Appreciate those whose vision placed it where it stands

Even for the holes and imperfections now

This old fence is a hiding place, the backdrop and comfort for garden treasures

It's once perfect symmetry gives way to weathered realities

Can barely live up to its intended purpose these days

Reminded of the care it needs in the surrendering

This old fence, it's time to let it go with tender and gentle care

A true gift, to yield and await something new and different

Something unknown to the eye, yet already held sacred in the heart

Perhaps a softened landscape, or a an unrevealed treasure

Something that will stand as true and steady

Giving way, with appreciation, for this old fence

English Ivy
Hedera helix

Zebra Dragonfly
Heliconius charithonia

Morning Light

Awaken
Slowly rise
Dawn a new day
Eyes catch You at Burning Bush
Glowing Red Heart
My own beating steady, thankful
To see You
On fire with color and light, vibrant red hue
Possibility and realization unite
Why were my eyes drawn to You?
What awareness do you support in this very moment?
I've done nothing, nothing much
Only glance and open
Revived by Your brilliance
Illuminating presence speaks softly, in the quiet and
stillness of day
Do you see it?
Do you see it all around?
Do I?
I do
Reminded now to stay awake
Only beginning
This new day
Yet all days before lead here

Support this very moment
Eyes open and alert
Don't miss it
Brilliant red will soon fade away
Leaves will fall and die
Within the earth they bleed and weep
In the eve of day
Where light dims to darkness
Red fiery heart beats on
Even in tranquil repose
Life vibrancy lives on
Dawning light awakens and clarifies
Soul's intention

Canyon Dreams

Canyon stillness
Notice everything wild and alive
Settles and calms
Nature's pace of ease
Invites expansion
Gentle movement

Canyon skies
Cottonwood fuzz on wind, drifts
White and light as air
To places far and wide
Detached and free
In flight with bird's eye view
Inner and outer realms discovered

Canyon Dreams
Travel far at rest and awake
To places distant and near
Reminded in stillness
Of what matters
The heart's journey
discovers love's buried treasures
Uncovered and brought to light
Canyon dreams

Bubbles and Prayers

When a body sinks into a pool of deep water
Bubbles rise; last bits of air float up like a circular prayer
Body sinking out of reach
Drowning before my very eyes
Though bubbles rise
Powerless to save you from your grief and despair
My arms not long enough to extend
Or strong enough to lift
Not wise enough to know what to do
Not even my place to try
Stand here conscious of our missed connection
Love held back or not fully understood
Missed for a lifetime, maybe more
Stand here, almost drowning in my own tears
Sending last bits of air floating to the surface
Bubbles and prayers
Circles of desire hoping to reach beyond to the heavens
No breath to give, only gasping and gurgling grief
Words from the depth of my heart leave my lips
Watching you go
Wishing you well
Thanking you for the ways you enriched my life
Bubbles travel beyond what I know
Prayers for your peace, and your comfort

Perhaps our bubbles will meet somewhere
In another time and place
Let them go and rise in hope
To meet there, smile and greet each other once again
With greater awareness
Bubbles and prayers

Warm Rivers

The hardest thing to do
Is nothing
Nothing at all
To feel helpless, powerless
To stand by while you slip away

Only the heart's hopes
Wanting to breathe
Life into your failing body
To send words and thoughts
That float in the air like magic

Transforming to hues of green and gold
Words to reach your heart and spirit
And let you know how special you are
Wanting to hold them there, let them hover
And have them surround you with love and acceptance

Words to sink to your very core
That might somehow bring you comfort and peace
Ease your withering body and tell you there is more
Much more than this
More than can be said in the confines of each day

How much you've touched our hearts
With your warm smiles
Your kind and bright nature has tinges of wildness;
Just enough to laugh. "Trouble"

And so
The hardest thing to do
Is stand distant and still
Present as each moment passes
Wanting to be useful
To give relief, yet not much at all to offer in that way
These words and intentions carefully sewn together and
may only reach you in dreams
A patchwork of many diverse hearts and stories
Coming together as one blanket for you
Pieced and stitched to offer you comfort and strength
Enough to cover you softly with loving kindness

Let this quilt hold all of your worries
And bring you to lasting peace
Let it comfort you while you fight this battle
And remind you of something greater than each of us
As we give thanks for your presence in our lives

Let this moment, as we honor your life, touch each of our hearts deeply
And remind us that life is forever teaching us to love more
Both in storms and smooth sailing
May this quilt hold all of our worries, may it give us peace in remembering you
And may it comfort us and remind us of something greater than each of us

Under warm and soft blanket let healing, warm rivers flow

A Mother's Love

A mother's love is often overlooked
Take care and time to look again
It is woven into the fabric of the ordinary
Sewn on with the buttons reattached to your favorite shirt
Quietly mixed into the ingredients of your favorite food
It is the soft touch on your fevered forehead
It is spoken softly, with tenderness
Or sometimes with a biting nip and growl intended to guide
and protect
It's there in the words which are carefully chosen in your
moment of need
It is creatively situated throughout the place you call your
home
Surrounding you with things that comfort
A place designed to make even a stranger feel welcome
and loved; a safe harbor
From the moment you were first in her belly
To the moment you step into who you are and beyond here
She is there loving you, in the only way she knows how
Sometimes it's not enough; though do not take the love she
can give for granted
Few if anyone know and love you this deeply

What do you know of who she is, of what she loves and values? Learn.

You may think she has no dreams

You may think what she does is insignificant, or comes easy without sacrifice

Challenge that thought

Forgive her for her human frailty, look beyond.

Look closely at all the seemingly ordinary acts of service

If you look deeply, you will feel her immense worth, you will see just how strong she is

Your will see her love and your heart will be full and grateful.

Strong Stock

I come from strong stock
And a long line of strong women too
Sometimes, strong women are silenced
Beaten down
Criticized
Enslaved by housework and thankless tasks
Held back and hidden
Surprisingly even by
And sometimes especially by
Their own mothers
And eventually by their own doing
It's not always safe to be a strong woman
Look at history
DNA remembers
The days when strong women were exiled
Used and abused
Burned in flames
Ostracized and bloodied
With threats and lifetimes of conditioning
On how to stay alive
Even after the need to condition and control have long
since disappeared
Still tongues are tempered and tamed
Behaviors patterns engrained
Stay small

Stay hidden

For intended survival

Fear lives long after threat is gone

Or motives are remembered

Leaves one believing I must be wrong to want more

Emphasis is put on attributes that serve

Put another's pleasure first, wait for someone else to move

Even when the cost is steep

Keep your mouth shut

Some attributes matter little in the end

Can be stolen or replaced when tired and old

External beauty weathers

She was so nice, such a good girl

Sweet one

What happened, why is she bitter and cold?

Bury alive our powers, Connection and gifts

All the while fire in the belly smolders

Secret wishes to be more, call and whisper in her ears

Perhaps by all the others, those before her

Generation upon generation of mothers, sisters, aunts and
daughters

A call to come alive again

Buried strength and talents awakened

DNA remembers these too

Wild spirit
Hidden sparks
Passion ignited
By the bands and tribe
By the burning need
Leaves one thinking, I am so honored

To be alive
Yes
To be strong
To be part of strong stock

Daffodil
Narcissus

Stand Up Now

It's time to push forward
This place has been increasingly confining
No longer welcoming or comfortable
It hurts too much to stay here

Fear is greater than the danger
Greet the Sun
Emerge
Like a flower, bursting forth

From the deep darkness of the dirt and earth
Who knows what will touch your face
Who knows what you will encounter or how it will feel
Simply open
Let the beauty of who you are simply be alive
Be it
Don't worry who notices
Exactly the right ones will

Tomorrow comes soon enough
Spring blooms will fade again
Live this moment
Reach for the sun and be just what you were created to be

Stand Up Now

"Peace and war begin at home. If we truly want peace in the world, let us begin by loving one another in our own families. If we want to spread Joy, we need for every family to have joy."
Mother Teresa, In My Own Words

The author and publisher are offering 10% of profits made from the sale of this book to promote, strengthen, and support domestic peace, equality, and joy at home through educational and empowerment programs intended to uplift and inspire families.

Peace…
In our own bodies
In the bodies around us
In our homes
In our churches
In our communities
In our states
In our regions
In our country
In our world

Joy…
In our own bodies
In the bodies around us
In our homes
In our churches
In our communities
In our states
In our regions
In our country
In our world

THE AUTHOR

Joan Scharff's words and photographs take us on a delightful journey and remind us to pay attention to the joy and beauty all around us.

Joan's poetry dives deep into the heart of things. With a vulnerable perspective, she generously shares a gift that nudges and nurtures the spirit forward on the journey of the heart. Joan's words inspire, connect and uplift readers as they travel the twists and turns of this creative life. Her insights reflect a deep sense of gratitude for the path.

When she's not working her 9 to 5, Joan can be found stealing moments in nature and communing with the flowers in her life. Joan lives in New Jersey with her son Michael, who she considers to be one of her greatest blessings, her silly roommate Jackie, and her impish dog Gracie, who she admits has her well-trained.

THE IMPISH DOG

Gracie is a thief who easily steals hearts and infuses life with much love and laughter.

Her highly intelligent and playful personality, as well as her incredibly cute face, spreads fun wherever her four paws carry her. She greets the loves of her life with much exuberance, bounce and joy.

Don't let Gracie's innocent face fool you though; she's bit of an imp with a strong and bossy side as well. Quite the huntress (just ask the skunks), Gracie's enthusiasm for the chase never ceases; though she also knows how to let sleeping dogs lie.

9 780984 033171